The Enchanted Tree of Crooked Lake

Happy Reading!
Andrea Longhurst
Sept, 2010

written by Rachel Longhurst
illustrated by Donna Pellegata
designed by Andrea Longhurst

With special thanks to...

… Grandma June for her royal wisdom.

… Donna for transforming what was held in my mind to delightful, royal illustrations.

… Andrea for her imaginative, creative royal talent.

… Krystin for her youthful royal wisdom and sunshine.

… my important royal editors.

… Crooked Lake, a charming 'fishpond' in Columbia City, Indiana.

As you read, see how many Crooked Lake bullfrogs you can find!

Printed at Millbrook Printing
Grand Ledge, Michigan USA

Enjoy our first book
"where my story begins"

RAK Publishing

First Printing 2010

Copyright 2010 all rights reserved

LCCN 200990841

ISBN 978-0-9767354-1-0

www.rakpublishing.com

For my
Knight in Shining Armor
and his
Cherished Queen!

As the sun rays pour in through the nature filled glass, I peacefully observe the world outside. My drowsy eyelids leisurely close and the stories held within my mind take me away to where my imagination plays.

And so begins a magical journey.

*O*nce upon a time…

*K*ing Karl and Queen June
were not the typical royalty that you might expect.

They didn't wear lavish clothes, glimmering jewelry
or crowns that looked too heavy for their heads to hold.

Their hair was a windswept gray, covered with floppy hats.
Their clothes were tattered denim jeans
and comfy flannel jackets,
with tee shirts underneath that had a hole or two.

But oh...

They are a special kind of royalty…
Who live on a special kind of lake…
Near a special kind of forest…
In a special kind of castle!

Crooked Lake is a charming fishpond surrounded by a magical forest.
Nestled deep within this forest, in a gnarled old tree,
is the castle of King Karl and Queen June.
They are the Crooked Lake royalty.

*O*verseeing
the Crooked Lake forest
from his treetop chimney nest is
the great osprey.
He protects all the creatures
that live within the forest.

*F*loating across the water,
just as the clouds do against the royal blue sky,
majestic wood duck sentries are on patrol.

*T*hose wishing to enter
the Crooked Lake forest
must gain permission before proceeding.

The heron and the kingfisher
are residents of this magical place, along with the
bluebirds who add their vibrant sapphire shades
against the forest green backdrop.

The hummingbirds also find themselves at home here
fluttering from blossom to blossom
savoring the delicious nectar of the flowers.

STUART
TRAIL

Life here is peaceful and the days progress
with a serene, routine splendor
of the simple pleasures the forest offers.

*O*ne of those pleasures
shared by King Karl and Queen June
is their cherished daily walk together
among the trees and the creatures of
the Cr_{oo}ke^d Lake forest.

Always traveling with them are Rafe, the powerful and majestic Bernese Mountain Dog and Otis, the whimsical, elfin-like cat who imagines himself as gigantic as Rafe!

During one early morning stroll down the delightful Crooked Lake forest path, King Karl, Queen June and their entourage…

...discover nature's wonder
as a doe and her newborn white-dappled fawn
lay drawing in the warmth
from the awakening, rising sun.

*S*ometimes Rafe and Otis have adventures of their own.
A favorite of Rafe's is following a woodland creek
as it meanders through the Crooked Lake forest.

He loves to run and splash in the cold water
and lap up a delicious drink. Otis wishes his fur were as thick as Rafe's
and his courage as GREAT, so he, too, could play in the creek.

As Rafe slowly gallops over the fallen logs next to the creek bed,
he barks to Otis, "We better keep moving on our way back to the tree castle.
King Karl and Queen June will be looking for us!"

While Rafe and Otis are off exploring on their own,
King Karl and Queen June returned from their morning walk
to relax with a mug of coffee
and a platter of delicious Toasty Warm Brown Bread
filled with plump raisins and nuts.

It was topped off with an
ENORMOUS
thick layer of cream cheese
spilling over the sides,
just as frosting would do
on a magnificent royal cake.

With tummies full from breakfast,
preparation for their daily fishing voyage began.
Queen June busily packed a picnic basket
with a lunch fit for royalty.

*K*ing Karl gathered his fishing poles, tackle boxes
and all that was needed for a successful day
of fishing on Cro₀ke d Lake.

"Queen June, where are Rafe and Otis?
I would like to leave soon for fishing,"
King Karl says as he is restless to be on his way.

With a shrug of her shoulders Queen June replies,
"I can only imagine where that pair has wandered!"

"*T*here you two are,"
Queen June smiles to Rafe and Otis
while they patiently wait on the dock.

"Permission to come aboard?"
she says when King Karl extends his
hand to escort her to the royal vessel.

As Rafe settles in for a lazy afternoon of slumber
and Otis takes his place at the bow of the royal vessel,
excitement builds as they cast off from shore.

What would they catch today?

"There's only one way to hook the BIG one!" King Karl bellows.
"Use my magical lure, THE BLACK JITTERBUG!
It will bring you luck fit for a queen!"

A lovely afternoon of fishing comes to a close.
The fireflies shimmer through
the Crooked Lake forest
and the Man in the Moon peeks his nose
over the horizon with his nightly glow,
illuminating the way to the dock.

*T*he June bugs and the bullfrogs
begin their evening concert with a cadence to march to
as the royal family carries their belongings back to the tree castle.

The osprey
settles in for his nightly guard duty
and the Sandman begins his evening rounds.
King Karl and Queen June,
along with Rafe and Otis,
snuggle in for a restful, royal slumber.

"Come close, Queen June,"
King Karl says,
"and let me put my 'paw'
around you tight and snug.

Sweet dreams to you!"

King Karl and Queen June's
Toasty Warm Royal Brown Bread

Ingredients:

4 cups .... Water

4 cups .... Raisins

2 cups .... Sugar

2 .... Eggs

2 tbsp .... Melted Butter

5 cups .... Flour

2 tsp .... Baking Soda

1 tsp .... Salt

4 cups .... Whole Walnuts

Directions for The Royal Batter:

With raisins and water in a sauce pan, bring water to a boil, and then turn off the heat and soak raisins for approximately 2 hours to create Royal, Plump Raisins!

Mix sugar, eggs and butter together.
(May be mixed by hand or with a mixer)
Add flour, baking soda, salt and the Royal, Plump Raisins (along with the water they were soaking in).

Mix well.
Stir in walnuts.
Spray 3 loaf pans with non-stick spray.
Pour equal amounts of Royal Batter into pans.
Bake in your oven at 325 degrees
for approximately 1-1/2 hours.

Royal Notes:

After using non-stick spray in loaf pans, for added flavor, sprinkle the pans with with cinnamon and sugar before adding the Royal Batter.
Top with a thick layer of royal cream cheese.
Freezes well.

 *Enjoy!*